number and
logic games
for preschoolers

First published in Great Britain in 2004 by
Hamlyn, a division of Octopus Publishing Group Ltd
2–4 Heron Quays, London E14 4JP

Distributed in the United States and Canada by
Sterling Publishing Co., Inc.
387 Park Avenue South
New York, NY 10016-8810

ISBN 0 600 61038 1

A CIP catalogue record for this book is available from the
British Library

Printed and bound in China

10 9 8 7 6 5 4 3 2 1

Acknowledgements
Executive editor Jane McIntosh
Editor Alice Tyler
Design manager Tokiko Morishima
Designer Ginny Zeal
Photography Adrian Pope and Peter Pugh Cook
Assistant production controller Nosheen Shan

number and
logic games
for preschoolers

Jane Kemp & Clare Walters
Consultant Dr Dorothy Einon

hamlyn

contents

foreword by Dr Dorothy Einon

Learning should be fun. Preschool children do not make any distinction between work and play or between playing and learning. All learning is embraced with enthusiasm as long as a child enjoys what he is doing.

Children learn about the world through play, but they don't always know how to organize or direct their play. This is why your child needs you to participate. All the games, tasks and activities in this book are designed for you and your child to do together. The learning may be serious, but the games are lighthearted – keep them that way. Talk, laugh and gossip as you play together, and offer guidance when it's needed.

Children tend to learn more effectively if they are allowed to run around and let off steam before they sit still to concentrate on a task. I've found that the best way to do this is to put on some music and let children run

around, shout and dance until the music stops. Young children, and boys in particular, find it difficult to sit still for long periods. One of the benefits of running around is that it gets blood pumping round the body, which brings a plentiful supply of oxygen to the brain.

You are the best judge of how long it is reasonable to expect your child to concentrate on a task. In my experience, an hour is a very long time for most three-year-olds. If you notice signs that your child is losing interest, fidgeting or becoming distracted, it may be time to stop.

Another good way of preparing for 'serious play' is to clear away any toys or other

Above: Children's love of water means that they will be naturally drawn to a water-based activity.

Right: Role-play creates an ideal environment for combining enjoyment with mental stimulation.

Left: Using familiar objects like bricks makes learning much more fun.

Below: An activity such as making a cake stimulates a child on many levels.

distractions that don't relate to the activity you're about to do. Small children are easily distracted and if there are competing activities they may find it hard to concentrate on the immediate task, particularly if it is a demanding one that requires a lot of thought. For this reason, it's also a good idea to turn off the radio or television.

One of the biggest aids to learning in children is self belief. It is amazing what children can achieve when they believe in their own competence and capabilities. This is why it's very important to praise a child for effort and make a fuss of success. Criticism undermines small children, damages their self-confidence and, ultimately, makes them feel that it is safer not to attempt something if they risk failure.

If your child starts misbehaving or being silly during an activity, rather than getting angry with him or telling him off, try saying: 'I can see you are not enjoying this – let's put it away for another day'. Putting pressure on your child to continue with something that doesn't interest him is counterproductive – research suggests

that young children who are pushed too hard, either in school or at home, often underachieve.

If your child habitually fidgets or misbehaves, you may need to practise sitting still and concentrating. Playing at the sink, reading stories, looking at books or sitting down with a drink and a biscuit for a chat are all good ways of doing this.

If your child struggles or responds badly to a particular activity, stop it and try an easier one. Look through the chapters in this book and find a game or activity that you think your child will enjoy. For example, he may not count building bricks but he may count toy cars. If your child is allowed to succeed at one activity he will be motivated to try other more difficult tasks. He should always feel that he has succeeded more often than he has failed.

Where possible, adapt a task or an activity to your child's interests and preferences. For example, if he won't sit still and draw shapes on paper, he might ride his bike around shapes drawn in water or chalk in a playground. Let the games stimulate your imagination too.

introduction

Your preschool child is learning something new every day. Sharing the pleasure of early learning with your child is exciting for you both, and even the simplest of activities can be used to introduce new concepts, such as shapes, counting and patterns.

When you try out the games and activities in this book, be guided by your child's mood. Choose a time when she's happy and relaxed. A good tip for capturing her interest is to start playing a game by yourself – an activity that's already underway can often tempt your child to join in. Don't be afraid to go back to games that you've played before – children learn a lot through repetition.

This book is packed with games and activities that will captivate your child and teach her all about the world of numbers and logic. Many of the skills she learns will help her with maths and reading in the future. Chapter One looks at first counting games and number recognition. You may want to keep returning to this chapter, as numeracy skills develop over time and your child's level of understanding increases each time she plays a game. Children under the age of three shouldn't play with small items, such as counters or dice, as there's a risk of choking. So be extra vigilant if younger brothers or sisters are playing alongside your preschool child.

Chapter Two is full of weighing and measuring activities, with lots of practical

everyday counting

Here are some examples of the counting activities that you and your child can do in the course of one day:

- Slowly count aloud while you get your child dressed – a useful distraction if she's keen on running off!

- Count the stairs as you go down to breakfast, the fingers of toast on her plate and the number of mugs on the table.

- Outside, count the number of houses before you turn the corner of your street, the number of letters to post and the number of dogs you pass.

- In the shops, count how many apples are in the bag or how many yogurts are in the pack.

- In the bath, count your child's ears, eyes, fingers and toes.

Below: Working through an exercise together provides enjoyment for both you and your child.

Below left: Music fires up a child's imagination and promotes a sense of well-being.

useful things to buy or collect

- Adhesive dots
- Card
- Children's glue
- Children's scissors
- Counters
- Felt-tip pens
- Finger paints
- Large crayons
- Large-squared paper
- Lined paper
- Modelling dough and shape cutters
- Old magazines for cutting up
- Paper fasteners
- Paper plates
- Peg board and pegs
- Plain paper
- Plastic model animals (for example, farm, zoo and sea animals and dinosaurs)
- Playing cards
- Poster paints
- Ribbon, string or wool
- Shape templates
- Sticky paper shapes
- Toy money
- Tracing paper
- Two dice
- Wooden bricks (different shapes, colours and sizes)

experiments to enjoy. Many focus on cooking in the kitchen and water play, so it's essential to supervise your child whenever she is near potential dangers, such as knives or a hot oven. Never leave a young child alone with water.

Shapes and sizes are introduced in Chapter Three – your child can have great fun comparing herself to the world around her. Young children are fascinated by shapes, and love the chance to show you that they recognize them. Once your child has grasped a knowledge of shapes and sizes she can use them in the patterns and sequences in Chapter Four.

You can improve your child's observation and memory skills with the sorting and matching games in Chapter Five, many of which can be played with everyday objects in your home. Anticipating what might happen next is a vital life skill, and the games in Chapter Six give your child practice in making logical predictions.

Spotting what's wrong with words or pictures also involves sophisticated logical thinking, so Chapter Seven is full of silly scenarios where your child has to identify the deliberate mistake – not always as easy as it might seem!

In Chapter Eight, the book concludes with a selection of musical games that include numbers and counting – children often find numbers easier to remember when they appear in a song or a rhyme and it also makes learning more enjoyable.

Developing confidence with numbers and logical skills gives your child a real head-start for school and adult life, so we hope you enjoy the activities together. Above all, have fun!

counting and
numbers

Little children love to count, even though they don't know what the numbers mean at first.

The games in this chapter help children learn to count up to five, up to ten and then back down again. There are also activities to encourage children to recognize written numbers.

toys' teatime

from 3 years

This teatime picnic game is a great way to introduce your child to counting.

- Choose two toys for a picnic tea.
- Lay out a toy tea-set and ask your child to give herself and each toy one cup, one saucer and one plate. Describe what she's doing: 'One for teddy, one for rabbit and one for you'.
- Make some mini-sandwiches and ask her to give each toy two sandwiches, talking through her actions.
- Do the same with other finger foods.
- Now help the toys enjoy their tea!

RESEARCH SAYS

' Teaching your child to count shows her how to group things according to whether they are alike or different. Children absorb information best when it is presented in a fun, practical way, like counting everyday objects. '

how many spots?
from 3 years

Drawing spots on ladybirds brings a visual dimension to counting.

- Draw several outlines of ladybirds.
- Colour them red together with your child.
- Now ask your child how many spots she thinks the first ladybird should have (five or less). Use a black pen to draw on the spots and then write the number alongside.
- Take it in turns to decide how many spots the second, and subsequent ladybirds, should have, and then draw them on.
- An older child can draw on her own spots and write her own numbers, perhaps by tracing over a faint line that you have drawn.

number story
from 3 years

Using numbers within a story can make them more meaningful to your child.

- Start with, 'Once upon a time there was a pretty bird who sat all alone on her empty nest'.
- 'One morning the bird looked into her nest and was very surprised to see one tiny egg lying on the twigs.' Hold up one finger or draw a nest containing one egg.
- 'The next morning the bird looked down again and was even more surprised to see another tiny egg lying on the twigs. She counted up her eggs: one, two.' Hold up two fingers or add another egg to the nest.
- Continue until the bird has five eggs in her nest.
- Finish by saying, 'One morning the pretty bird heard some cheeping ... and, looking down into her nest, she saw five hungry little chicks just waiting for their dinner!'

which one has six?

from 4 years

This game encourages accuracy in counting.

- Divide a piece of paper into four sections.
- Draw three balls in the first section, six boats in the second section, four flowers in the third section and two fish in the fourth section.
- Together with your child, count the number of objects in each section and ask her to point to the one that contains six.
- Make the game harder for your child by increasing the number of choices.
- An older child can draw extra objects so that all of the sections contain six items.

lucky throw

from 4 years

Using a die helps your child to recognize patterns of numbers.

- Show your child a die and explain how each side shows a different number of dots from one to six.
- Take turns to throw the die and count how many dots are showing.
- When your child is confident with this, get another die and throw together to see who gets the highest number.
- See how many throws it takes until you both get the same number.
- An older child can try counting both sets of dots on the dice.

match mine
from 3 years

Can your child count out the same number of objects as you?

- Find a range of small objects, such as counters, bricks, buttons or beads. Give half of each to your child and keep half for yourself.

- Put down two bricks, counting them out as you do so. Ask your child to put down a button beside each brick.

- Gradually increase the number of objects you put down and get your child to match that number (using a different object). You can also swap so that your child goes first and you match her number of objects.

- If your child finds this game difficult, suggest she puts each one of her items exactly next to each one of yours.

RESEARCH SAYS

❝ There are two elements to counting: recognizing the sound of an individual number and its written symbol, and linking this to a specific quantity of objects. It is putting the two together that is difficult. ❞

houses in a row

from 3 years

Making a concertina street may help your child to recognize written numbers.

- Take a strip of paper and fold it into a concertinaed square. Before you unfold the paper, make a diagonal cut from halfway up each side towards the centre at the top. Now unfold the paper to reveal a series of house shapes joined together.

- Ask your child to draw a big door on each house. Then write on the door numbers. Count how many houses there are, pointing to the door numbers as you go.

- Ask your child to decorate the doors and houses, then put them on the fridge with magnets, or make a hole at each end and hang them up.

RESEARCH SAYS

❛ Children learn well when matching the words 'one', 'two', 'three' to a sequence of objects. Encouraging your child to point to each object and count in this way will facilitate his learning. ❜

animal extras
from 4 years

Drawing different size groups of objects helps young children to remember numbers.

- Draw a kitten with three balls of wool beside it. Ask your child how many balls of wool the kitten has to play with.

- Draw a horse with five apples beside it. How many has it got to eat?

- Draw a dog and tell your child you're going to give the dog six bones. Ask him to count the bones as you draw, and to stop you when you've drawn enough.

- If your child finds this easy, ask him to draw the objects for animals himself: four carrots for a rabbit, seven eggs for a hen or ten twigs for a bird's nest.

match the pictures
from 4 years

Help your child to practise his counting skills by getting him to link matching sets of objects.

- Draw six circles. Draw four apples in one circle and four pencils in another (not too near the first circle). Draw two more matching circle pairs (for example, five oranges and buttons, and seven books and balloons).

- Ask your child to draw lines joining the circles that contain the same number of objects.

- Repeat this game, adding an extra circle of objects that doesn't have a matching partner. Ask your child if he can spot the odd one out.

number dominoes
from 4 years

Playing dominoes is a great way to get your child excited about numbers.

- Cut out 28 cards of 8 x 4 cm (3 x 1.5 in). Draw a line down the middle of each card to create two squares. On the first seven cards put one dot on each left-hand square. On each right-hand square, put dots from one to seven.

- On the next six cards put two dots on each left-hand square. On the right-hand square, put dots from two to seven. Continue to reduce the cards by one each time. Your final card should have seven dots in each square.

- Shuffle the completed cards. Give yourself and your child eight each and put the remainder in a pile.

- Lay down the first card. Your child must match the number of dots at either end of your card with one of his own. If he can't, he must take a card from the pile. Then it's your turn. The first person to use up all their cards wins.

race me!
from 4 years

This first board game is a fun way to encourage your child to count up to six.

- Draw a wiggly path of two fairly wide parallel lines.

- Divide the path into 50 or so squares. Make the first square the starting point, the last the finishing post, and number the others in between.

- Add some lucky moves, such as, 'You've landed on a treasure trove, move on two squares', and some unlucky moves, such as, 'There's a rock on the path, go back one square'.

- Put two counters on the starting point and take turns to throw a die, moving the counters as many squares forward as the dots on the die show.

- The first person to the finishing post is the winner.

fruity fractions

from 4½ years

This game is a practical way to introduce your child to the concept of fractions.

- Explain to your child that many objects can be divided into equal portions so that two or more people can share them.
- Cut an apple in half and ask him how many people could have a piece.
- Cut the apple into quarters and ask your child how many people could share it now.
- If your child finds this easy, set out the segments of an orange and ask him to count them.
- Try giving your child a small bunch of grapes and asking him to share it between you so that you each have the same number of grapes.

RESEARCH SAYS

❝Preschoolers only take in two to three objects at a glance (adults take in about seven). More objects must be counted to ascertain how many there are. Objects arranged in specific patterns, such as the dots on dominoes, can help at-a-glance number recognition.❞

up to ten and back
from 4 years

This game
encourages
your child to
use her fingers
to count with.

- Using a non-toxic and non-permanent pen, write the numbers one to ten on your child's fingertips. Start with one on her left thumb, moving on to six on the little finger of her right hand and ending with ten on her right thumb.

- Ask her to curl her fingers up in a ball. Start counting and ask her to raise the appropriate finger as you say each number. When you get to ten all her fingers should be showing.

- Now ask your child to fold down each finger as you count back down. When you reach one, all her fingers should be hidden.

RESEARCH SAYS

❝ **When first learning to count, your child chants numbers as she would nursery rhymes – by simple imitation and repetition. To understand a number's meaning, she must learn that five is one more than four and one less than six.** ❞

blast off!

from 3 years

Your child will love the anticipation of counting back from ten as her rocket gets ready to blast off into space.

- Make a rocket from a cardboard tube with a cone of card on top. Let your child decorate it.
- Cut out 11 cards and write a number on each from one to ten, plus the words 'blast off!' on the final card.
- Put the cards in a pile in numerical order with ten on the top and the 'blast off!' card at the bottom.
- Hold the rocket on the floor while your child turns over the cards and counts downwards.
- When she gets to 'blast off!' make the rocket soar up in the air.

one cunning mouse

from 3 years

This simple story is an amusing introduction to the concept of counting down.

'Once upon a time there were five galloping horses.
The five galloping horses were chasing four racing pigs.
The four racing pigs were chasing three speedy dogs.
The three speedy dogs were chasing two fat cats.
The two fat cats were chasing one cunning mouse.
But what happened to that one cunning mouse?
Why, he ran squeak, squeak, squeak, into his hole and
*   never came out again!'*

- Use finger movements as you count down, and then count how many animals there are altogether.

textured numbers
from 3 years

Decorating a number with bright colours can help your child to remember it.

- Choose a number – your child's age is a good choice – draw its shape on a piece of card and cut it out. The larger the better.
- Scrunch up some brightly coloured tissue paper into small balls.
- Cover one side of the card with children's glue and stick on the tissue paper balls.
- Let the card dry, then punch a hole in the top, thread it with string and hang it in your child's bedroom.
- Repeat with other numbers using a variety of materials for decoration. Make a colour collage from magazine pictures, or use shiny foil, newspaper or cotton wool.

my special numbers
from 4 years

Every child has numbers that are special to him and it's fun to record them in a book.

- Fold over some sheets of paper to make a mini-book. Stick a photograph of your child on the front, then add his name and the words: 'My special numbers'.
- On the first page write: 'I am four years old', making the number larger than the words. Ask your child to colour in the number and draw a picture of himself on the page.
- On the next page write: 'I was born on the ... of ...' (insert the date and month of his birthday), again making the numbers bigger than the words so that your child can decorate them.
- On the next page write: 'My door number is ...', 'Our house has ... bedrooms', 'I have ... soft toys' and so on.
- On the back page write: 'And my favourite number is ...!'.

so tasty!

from 3 years

Edible numbers
are not only fun
to make (and eat!),
they also teach
your child what
different numbers
look like.

- Buy a packet of plain biscuits, a packet of writing icing and some raisins.

- On the first biscuit write the number one in icing. Add another small dollop of icing at the bottom and stick a raisin to it.

- Take another biscuit and write the number two in icing. Stick two raisins underneath.

- Continue like this until you've reached five. Then line all the biscuits up in a row from one to five, ready to eat.

RESEARCH SAYS

❝ Children have an innate awareness of quantity. Think how upset your child would be if you gave him one cookie less than his friend! When you teach your child about numbers, you are directing this natural interest. ❞

my number frieze

from 3 years

This decorative number frieze makes numbers part of your child's everyday environment.

- Cut out five pieces of card measuring 15 x 20 cm (6 x 8 in).

- Cut out magazine pictures of, for example, one person, two cars, three dogs, four cushions and five plates.

- Write the number one large on the first card and ask your child to stick on the picture of the person. Repeat with the other cards, matching numbers and pictures.

- Put the cards up around your child's bedroom in numerical order. Alternatively, make a book with them.

- Add more number cards when you feel that your child is ready.

spot the number

from 3 years

Focusing on one number helps to clarify it in your child's mind.

- Choose a 'number of the day' and draw it on a piece of card for your child to see and hold.

- During the day point out that number every time you see it: on car licence plates, doors, buses, shops, petrol stations, price labels and so on.

- Surprise your child by cutting out the number from a slice of bread or forming it from some mashed potato. At the end of the day talk about all the different places you saw the number.

- Sing a song or read a bedtime story to your child that involves the number, such as Three Little Pigs or Snow White and the Seven Dwarfs.

mini-bingo
from 4 years

Playing bingo is an exciting way to introduce number matching to your child.

- Cut out two rectangular pieces of card and divide each one into two rows of five squares. In each square write random numbers from one to ten.

- Now make two more boards bearing exactly the same numbers as the first two. Cut this second set up into individual squares and put them in a bag (one that you can't see through).

- Give your child one board and keep the other yourself.

- Take turns to pick a square from the bag. If it matches a number on your board, lay it over the top of that number. If it doesn't, put it back in the bag.

- The first person to cover their board with squares wins and shouts 'bingo!'.

RESEARCH SAYS

❝ Showing your child how adults use basic maths helps her to make the connection between the counting games that she plays for fun and the usefulness of applying numbers to everyday life. ❞

weighing and measuring

Children enjoy making discoveries about themselves and the world around them.

The weighing and measuring activities in this chapter are hands-on games that use everyday objects. They give your child the opportunity to use numbers in a very practical way. They also encourage observation skills as your child explores the concepts of length, weight and capacity.

pizza maths
from 4 years

Most children love making pizza and it offers lots of opportunities for practical maths.

- Buy a large, ready-made pizza base, tomato purée, grated cheese and a selection of toppings, for example, olives, sliced tomatoes, strips of pepper or pepperami slices.

- Spread the purée on the pizza base and sprinkle with grated cheese.

- Use a knife to lightly score the pizza base into slices.

- Ask your child to add the toppings so that each slice gets an equal amount.

fruity cocktails
from 4 years

This fruit juice cocktail game helps your child to understand the concept of capacity.

- Gather together three clear plastic cups and a measuring jug.

- Decide with your child which juices to mix in your cocktail, for example, orange, apple and cranberry.

- Pour a small amount of orange juice into one cup, apple juice into the second, and cranberry in the third. Now ask your child to complete the cocktail by adding roughly equal amounts of the other juices to each cup.

- Let your child pour the three drinks into the jug, first guessing how far up the jug the cocktail will come.

- For an older child, vary the amounts of juice you put in each cup, using a measuring jug for accuracy.

let's make cakes

from 4 years

Your child learns about weighing and measuring with this simple fairy cake recipe – but make sure she stays away from the hot oven!

- Gather together eggs, sugar, flour and butter.

- Ask your child to weigh 60 g (approximately 2 oz) of each ingredient. Alternatively, let a single egg be their measuring guide – crack it into a measuring jug, check the level, then measure the same amount each of sugar, flour and butter.

- Cream together the butter and sugar with a wooden spoon. Mix in the egg a little at a time. Then add the flour gradually.

- Spoon the mixture into cake cases, and bake in a medium oven for 12–15 minutes.

- An older child may be able to suggest what would happen if she used too much or too little of any of the ingredients.

RESEARCH SAYS

❝ Activities such as baking provide valuable lessons not just about weights and measures but also about breaking a task down into stages that must be performed in a set sequence (children don't naturally look at activities in terms of sequences). ❞

funny feet
from 4 years

Teach your child a fun way to measure things using his own feet.

- Ask your child to stand without shoes on a piece of paper or card.
- Draw round the outline of his feet and help him to cut out the shapes.
- Ask your child to use the cut-out feet to measure familiar objects, such as a table – how many steps can the feet make across the surface?
- Use the feet to measure longer distances, such as the width of a room or the garden.
- A younger child will enjoy making lots of feet and placing them end-to-end, where you can number them and help him to count them.

that's me!
from 4 years

Help your child to learn about length and numbers using his own body.

- Use a large piece of paper, such as wallpaper, to draw around the outline of your child's body.
- Look at the outline together and ask your child whether his arms are longer or shorter than his legs, and how many fingers and toes he has.
- Ask your child to draw in his eyes, nose, mouth and hair, then clothes (including buttons).
- Count your child's features together and describe how eyes, ears, arms and legs come in pairs, whereas we have only one nose and mouth.
- Help your child cut out the outline of his body and stick it on his bedroom wall.

how tall am I?
from 4 years

Your child will love making first discoveries about his height.

- Find a ball of wool and a pair of child-safe scissors.
- Ask your child to stand up straight by a wall or lie on the floor. Tuck the loose end of the wool under his heel, or tape it down.
- Unravel the wool until it's at the top of your child's head. Cut it so that you have a piece that's the same height as your child.
- Encourage your child to use the wool to compare his height with other things in your home such as the height of a door or chest of drawers, the width of a stair or the length of his bed.

RESEARCH SAYS

❝ Central to your child's understanding of numbers is the discovery that things can be 'bigger than' or 'smaller than', 'taller than' or 'shorter than'. Measuring familiar objects using an improvised ruler facilitates this discovery. ❞

giant in the garden
from 3 years

This game uses imaginative ways to measure an area of floor or ground.

- Tell your child that you're both giants who take enormous footsteps.
- Count how many giant steps it takes you to get across the living room floor or garden.
- Now you're going to be dainty pixies who take little skipping steps. How many steps does it take this time?
- Next try being frogs or rabbits who have to hop, or birds taking pigeon steps.
- Count out loud together as you go.
- To vary the game, mark out a large circle with string, and see how many steps or hops it takes to get around your circle.

RESEARCH SAYS

❝Children find it difficult to hold more than one comparison in mind at a time. Tasks that involve looking at the sizes of several items at once encourage your child to make multiple comparisons.❞

a neater bookshelf
from 3 years

This useful activity encourages your child to arrange objects in height order.

- Tell your child that you're both going to tidy up her bookshelves.
- Look at the shelves and ask your child to point out the tallest and the shortest books.
- Help your child to re-order the books so they're all in height order.
- Congratulate her on having a neat and tidy bookshelf!

house hunt
from 4 years

A tour of your home helps your child to make visual comparisons of room sizes.

- Pretend that you and your child are explorers, setting off to discover things about where you live.
- Ask your child to lead you to the smallest room and then to the biggest room in your house.
- Ask your child to take you to the narrowest part of your house.
- Are there any rooms that are taller than others?
- Now count how many rooms, doors and windows there are in your house.
- An older child may enjoy preparing a list of things to look out for, and ticking them off as she goes.

the great wall
from 4 years

This easy building game encourages first counting skills.

- Gather together your child's bricks – the more the better.
- Ask him to build a wall that stretches all the way across his room, or if you have enough bricks, all the way around his room.
- Count how many bricks there are in the wall by marking off groups of ten.
- Alternatively, build a shorter wall with several rows of bricks, and count up how many rows there are.

up the stairs
from 3 years

This activity demonstrates how height can be increased in easy steps.

- Find 40 square construction bricks. Help your child to build a square base measuring four by four bricks.
- Add another layer of bricks to the base but miss out a row to create a stair.
- Add another layer of bricks but miss out two rows to create a second stair. Finally, add just one row of bricks to create a third stair.
- Ask your child to help one of his toys climb the steps, counting them as he goes.
- An older child may enjoy making a tall, narrow staircase only two bricks wide but ten bricks long.

toy parade
from 3 years

Your child will love spotting the differences between his favourite toys.

- Gather together a selection of your child's toys at random.
- Ask him to pick out any two of them and put them side by side.
- Now ask him to tell you which one is bigger and which one is taller or longer.
- If he has lots of toys of one particular type, such as teddies or cars, ask him to line them up in order of size.
- Alternatively, help him to sort all his toys into groups – soft toys, cars, puzzles and so on – and then count how many there are in each group.

RESEARCH SAYS

6 Large groups of objects are difficult for your child to quantify because he cannot see at a glance how many there are. Dividing objects into smaller groups makes counting and comparing activities more manageable. 9

splish, splash, splosh
from 3 years

Pouring water is a fun way for children to learn about how liquids are contained.

- Your child can play this game in the bath, at the sink or with a large bowl of water. Stay with your child all the time he's playing with water.

- Give him a selection of things he can use for pouring water: a small plastic jug, a beaker, a yogurt pot with a small hole in the bottom, a sieve, a funnel and a small plastic bottle.

- Ask your child which things hold water and which let it pass through. Talk about how quickly or slowly the water passes through the objects with holes in them.

- An older child may enjoy finding out how many times he can fill up a small beaker with the water from one plastic bottle.

RESEARCH SAYS

❛ **Young children find it hard to grasp how liquids occupy spaces. Until around the age of six, if shown a tall glass and a short glass, each containing an equal amount of water, they will always believe that the tall glass holds more water.** ❜

which has more?

from 4½ years

This is a quick way to introduce your child to the fascinating properties of liquids and the concept of volume.

- Find a measuring jug and two transparent cups – one that's short and wide, the other tall and narrow.
- Pour 100 ml (3.5 fl oz) of water or juice into the measuring jug, and show your child the mark the liquid has reached on the side of the jug.
- Pour the liquid into the short cup.
- Measure out another 100 ml (3.5 fl oz) of liquid and pour this into the tall cup.
- Put the cups side by side and ask your child if he thinks one contains more than the other, or if they're both the same.

it's pouring!

from 3 years

Play this game to discover the different rates at which solids and liquids can be poured.

- Collect a number of household ingredients such as salt, rice and dried lentils, and pour equal portions into plastic cups.
- Add cups of water and dry play-sand to your collection.
- Ask your child to pour each item in turn through a funnel, colander, sieve or a plastic pot with a hole in the bottom.
- Talk about how water pours very quickly, followed by salt and sand, and then rice and lentils. Do any of the ingredients get stuck? What happens if the ingredients get wet?
- An older child can use a timer – you can help him to record his findings on paper.

roundabout

from 4 years

This is a simple introduction to the idea of measuring solid objects.

- Help your child to cut a piece of string around 15–20 cm (6–8 in) long.

- Collect a selection of objects, such as an orange, a jar, a book, a small box and a beaker.

- Ask your child to compare how far the string will go round each one.

- He can also try measuring your wrist and ankle and comparing them to his own.

who's the ruler?

from 3 years

Your child will enjoy making independent observations and using a grown-up tool.

- Show your child a short ruler.

- Send him on a mission to find three things that are longer than the ruler, for example, a cushion, a soft toy and a box of cereal.

- Next he has to find three things that are shorter than the ruler, for example, a teaspoon, an apple and a CD.

- Point out other household objects and ask him to discover if they're longer or shorter than the ruler.

wiggly jiggly
from 4 years

This simple measuring activity helps your child to understand that objects of the same length can look very different.

- Cut two equal lengths of ribbon. Arrange one in a wiggly line and the other in a straight line.

- Ask your child which of the two pieces of ribbon he thinks is the longest.

- Straighten the wiggly piece of ribbon to show him that both pieces of ribbon are the same length. Let your child repeat the exercise by himself.

- Try making other shapes, such as circles, coils, squares or triangles with the pieces of ribbon.

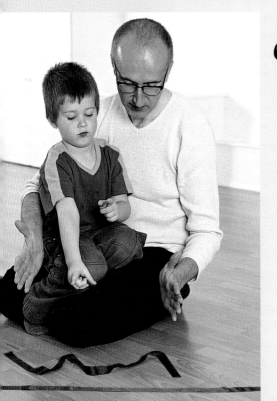

RESEARCH SAYS

❛ **Research suggests children do not have a concept of measurement until they learn to put things into sequences, for example small, medium, large. Try to do these tasks systematically because this will help them to understand.** ❜

weigh it up

from 3 years

This is a hands-on way to discover weights and measures.

- Gather a variety of small items from around the house or garden, making sure that some are heavier than others.

- Ask your child to become a human weighing scale, simply by holding her hands out to the sides.

- Place a light object, such as a leaf, in one palm.

- Place a heavier object, such as a pebble, in the other palm.

- Ask your child to judge which is the heavier item.

- This game also works well if your child closes her eyes so she has no visual clues as to which object is heavier or lighter.

RESEARCH SAYS

❝Some mental comparisons can't be made until your child has developed an appropriate level of memory. When this level is reached, you can help her to practise her comparison skills by encouraging her to make lots of visual comparisons of objects at home and outdoors. ❞

park life
from 3 years

An outing can encourage your child to use her powers of observation to judge weights.

- Go for a walk in the park with your child.
- If there's a pond, ask her if she can see which duck looks like the biggest and heaviest. Are there any smaller or lighter birds?
- Look at the plants and trees. Ask your child to find something that's very light, such as a twig, or to point out something that's very heavy, such as a tree.
- Look out for animals and birds in the trees. Are they light or heavy? What would happen to a thin branch if a big animal climbed on it?
- Pick up a stick and ask your child to bring you something that's heavier and something that's lighter.

let's get together
from 4 years

This game reinforces your child's understanding of how weights vary.

- Draw a line down the centre of a piece of paper.
- On either side of the line draw some heavy things, such as a lorry, an elephant and a hippo, and some light things, such as a pin, a feather and a bubble.
- Ask your child to draw lines that connect pairs of light things and pairs of heavy things.
- Ask your child if she can think of any more especially heavy or light things, and then draw pictures of them together.

shapes
and sizes

Shapes are a key concept in maths, but as far as your child is concerned they're just lots of fun.

With your encouragement he'll quickly learn to recognize and name basic shapes, and will find shapes such as stars and hearts fascinating. When he starts to learn about size, he will enjoy making comparisons that relate directly to himself – whether he is bigger or smaller, taller or shorter than other people in your family!

where's the square?

from 4 years

Play this game to stimulate your child's visual memory of shapes.

- Draw, colour and cut out a circle, a square, a triangle and a rectangle.
- Line them up and show them to your child.
- Explain that you're going to take one of the shapes away. Ask her to close her eyes and take away the square.
- Push the remaining shapes together, then ask your child to open her eyes and tell you which shape is missing.
- Play the game again, taking away a different shape. You can make the game easier by using fewer shapes, or more difficult by adding more complex shapes such as diamonds, pentagons and hexagons.

making shapes

from 4½ years

This shape-making activity helps your child to understand how many sides shapes have and that not all shapes have sides of equal length.

- Cut out a selection of thin paper strips, making most of equal length and a few shorter or longer.
- Show your child how to make a square from four pieces of paper that are equal in length. See if she can make one without help.
- Ask her to make a rectangle from two long and two short pieces of paper.
- Ask her to make a triangle, first from three pieces of paper that are equal in length and then from three pieces of different lengths.
- Can she make a diamond or even a pentagon?
- Point out which shapes you can't make with straight sides, such as a circle or an oval.

shaping up
from 3 years

Children find it immensely satisfying to create their own simple shapes.

- Using soft modelling dough, help your child to roll out a long, thin sausage.

- Show her how to form a circle by joining the ends of the sausage together.

- Next, make the sausage into a triangle or a square.

- If your child finds this difficult, draw the shapes clearly on a piece of paper, and ask her to place the modelling-dough sausage over your outlines.

- Once she's confident, try more complicated shapes such as a diamond or star.

- An older child will enjoy counting how many sides each shape has, or even measuring and comparing the length of each side.

RESEARCH SAYS

❝ A two-year-old is unlikely to be able to match a three-dimensional shape with a two-dimensional one, such as a sphere with a circle. Even at the age of three, this task is difficult and will need a lot of practice. ❞

big square

from 4 years

This simple game shows your child how joining shapes together can create new ones.

- Gather together some square and triangular bricks.

- Ask your child to fit four square bricks together. Describe how he's created one big square from four small ones.

- Ask your child to add more square bricks around the perimeter to make an even bigger square.

- Set an older child the challenge of making a small square from two triangular bricks or a bigger one from eight. See if he can make a rectangle from six square bricks. Which bricks – and how many – does it take to make a house shape with a triangular roof?

RESEARCH SAYS

6 **Learning about shapes and objects is more complex than it might seem. Your child may be able to point out a rectangle and a book but he will have difficulty grasping the concept that the book is also a rectangle.** 9

match the brick
from 3 years

Help your child to recognize identical objects by size, shape and colour.

- Gather an assortment of different shaped bricks.
- Choose a cube and hold it up for your child to look at.
- Ask your child to find a brick that is identical in terms of shape, size and colour.
- Give him clues such as 'its sides are all the same size', or 'this one looks like an arch'.
- Make the game easier or harder by limiting or extending the choice of bricks.

pick a brick
from 3 years

Encourage your child to explore the different properties of three-dimensional shapes.

- Empty a box of mixed bricks on to the floor.
- Ask your child to pick out three or four bricks.
- Experiment with each one to discover what it can do. Can you roll it along the floor? Can you stack it on top of anything else? Can you put anything on top of it? Can you slide a pencil underneath?
- Point out any surprises, for example, cylinders can't be stacked on their sides, but when they're upright you can pile them high.

colour my shape
from 3 years

This game helps your child to identify shapes, even when they're of different sizes.

- Draw a selection of circles, squares and triangles of the same size. Find some crayons or coloured pencils.

- Choose a colour and/or pattern for each shape, for example, red spots for circles, blue stripes for squares and green zig-zags for triangles.

- Ask your child to colour the shapes in the appropriate colours and/or patterns.

- Now draw the same shapes but in different sizes. Ask your child to colour them in again.

- To make the game easier for younger children, draw each shape in a row.

paper snowflakes
from 4 years

This creative activity teaches your child how to make a range of complex shapes and designs by folding and cutting paper.

- Cut out a circle of paper, then count aloud 'one, two, three, four' as you fold it over four times to make a fan shape.

- Using child-safe scissors, show your child how to make snips in the top edge and down either side of the fan.

- Let him open up the paper. Point out how the snips have created a snowflake shape.

- Ask him to make several snowflakes and compare the designs of each one.

picture this
from 3 years

This activity will help to improve your child's confidence at recognizing shapes.

- Look at a picture from a magazine or a picture book.
- Ask your child if he can spot any familiar shapes within the picture, for example, square windows, a circular wheel or a rectangular table.
- Count how many there are of each shape.
- Draw a picture of your house and see how many familiar shapes you can include.
- Try and draw a picture using only one shape, for example, a robot drawn from only squares.

RESEARCH SAYS

6 Pointing out shapes within a picture is difficult for small children. For example, your child may be able to point out the petals on a picture of a flower but unable to point out anything that is oval-shaped. 9

can you feel it?

from 4½ years

Children love this very physical way of learning to sense shapes.

- Explain that you're going to trace the outline of a shape on your child's palm.

- Ask her to close her eyes and hold out her hand. Lightly trace a circle.

- If she can't guess what the shape is, let her watch while you trace the circle again.

- Try tracing other shapes. Vary the game by tracing a shape on your child's back. Or let her keep her eyes open while you draw the shape in the air.

RESEARCH SAYS

❛ Learning to recognize shapes in drawing and shape-sorting games helps your child to recognize letters and words and is a valuable pre-reading skill. ❜

double up
from 3 years

Encourage your child to observe shapes carefully by copying your pictures.

- Cut out some simple shapes from coloured paper.
- Make a picture out of the shapes. For example, a tree from a rectangle and a triangle, or a house from a square with a triangle on top.
- Ask your child if she can copy the picture you've made, using identical shapes.
- If this is difficult, give her the appropriate shapes to get her started. If it's easy, get her to make a picture for you to copy.

picture scene
from 4 years

This exercise encourages your child to build imaginative pictures from familiar shapes.

- Cut out an assortment of shapes from coloured paper or use ready-made gummed shapes.
- Show your child how to stick the shapes on to paper to create a picture.
- Ask her to make a boat from triangles, a house from squares or a flower from circles.
- Now ask her to make pictures from multiple shapes. Encourage your child to create a background to her picture. Together, count how many shapes she has used.

where's my baby?

from 3 years

This favourite theme of 'mothers and babies' helps your child learn about size and number.

- On a piece of paper draw simple pictures of a cow, sheep, fish, horse and chicken.
- Somewhere else on the paper, draw the baby animals that belong to each creature.
- Ask your child to draw a line connecting each baby to its mother. Who is bigger – the mother or the baby?
- To make it more challenging, include animals with 'unusual' babies, such as butterflies and caterpillars, or frogs and tadpoles.
- Count how many animals there are altogether.

sizewise!

from 3½ years

This fun activity helps your child to understand height and age differences between people.

- Draw simple pictures of your family or friends that reflect their respective heights.
- Help your child to cut out the pictures, then lay them in a row and count them.
- Ask your child if he can put them in height order. Help him by asking, 'Who is the tallest? Who comes next? Who is the smallest?'.
- Alternatively, arrange the family in age order. Has anyone moved places?
- Let your child colour in the pictures and stick them down.
- He will also enjoy playing this game with cut-out animals or plants and trees.

who's hungriest?
from 4 years

Familiar themes, such as dinner time, make it easy for your child to understand the concept of small and large portions.

- Draw two big plates and one small plate in a row on a piece of paper. Alternatively, use paper plates.
- The first plate is for dad, the second is for mum and the third is for your child.
- Ask your child to draw some sausages on each plate. The first plate should have three sausages, the second should have two and the third should have one.
- Now ask your child to draw a large, medium and small portion of chips and peas on the respective plates.

RESEARCH SAYS

❝ Children's drawings give us a fascinating insight into how they see the world. Even when your child masters shape, the relative sizes of the flowers and the house tell us that there is still much to learn. ❞

busy caterpillar
from 3 years

Encourage shape recognition and counting with this simple but satisfying exercise.

- Draw eight to ten circles on a piece of card, cut them out and help your child to colour them in a variety of bright shades.

- Draw a face on the first circle and help your child to stick it on a large piece of paper. Add antennae.

- Stick the other circles on to the piece of paper so that they overlap in a wiggly line.

- Draw two legs on each circle.

- Help your child count how many circles make up the caterpillar, and how many legs it has altogether.

busy box
from 4 years

This activity shows your child that it's possible to create a 3-D box from a 2-D shape.

- Draw four fairly large squares of the same size in a straight line on a piece of card. Draw an extra square on either side of the second square in the line. You now have a cross shape.

- Cut out the cross shape, fold the creases, then use a hole-punch to make a hole on each side of the four outermost squares.

- Fold the squares so that they form a box with a lid.

- Help your child thread a piece of ribbon or wool through the holes.

- Put a small treat, treasure or toy inside the box and then tie the ribbon to keep it safe.

six sides
from 4½ years

Challenge your child by letting him experiment with more complex shapes.

- Cut out a hexagon (a shape with six equal sides) from a piece of card. Draw round the hexagon ten times on a piece of paper.

- Ask your child to colour each hexagon a different colour and then to cut them out carefully.

- Ask him to make different patterns with the hexagons by fitting them together in a honeycomb.

- Make more hexagons but this time ask your child to cut each hexagon into triangular sections like cake slices and colour each one differently. Count how many triangles there are in each hexagon.

RESEARCH SAYS

❝ Understanding how shapes tessellate, or the difference between shapes of different dimensions, are important maths skills. Although girls equal or surpass boys in maths tests, more boys than girls have precocious mathematical ability. ❞

watch me grow
from 3 years

Play this fantasy game in which your child imagines growing from a tiny seed into a tall tree.

- Ask your child to curl up on the floor and pretend that she is a tiny seed.
- Tell her that the sun is shining and the rain is falling on her. It's time to uncurl – ask her to stand up very slowly and stretch her arms towards the sky. When she is upright, tell your child to imagine that she is a big, strong tree.
- Repeat the exercise but pretend that your child is a chick hatching out of an egg and growing into a chicken.
- Talk to your child about how sizes change and how babies get bigger as they get older. Show her something that she can reach now that she couldn't reach when she was smaller, such as a door handle.

hands and feet
from 4½ years

This game shows your child how the area of your hand holds more than hers.

- Help your child to draw round her hand on large-squared paper. Then draw round your own hand on another piece.
- Count how many whole squares fall within the outline of her hand and how many in yours. Which hand has the most?
- Ask your child to colour in all the whole squares in one colour, and the partial squares in another colour.
- Try the same experiment with your and your child's foot.

I'm a star!

from 3 years

Making shapes with her body is a novel way to help your child to visualize and remember them.

- Tell your child she's amazingly bendy and can make herself into almost any shape she likes.

- Stand in front of a mirror and ask your child to become a star with her arms above her head and her feet positioned wide apart.

- Now ask her to be a ball by crouching down and tucking her head between her knees.

- Now ask her to make the shape of a pencil by standing up as straight and tall as she can.

- Finally, ask her to become a triangle shape by bending forward and putting her hands flat on the floor so that her body forms a wide 'v'.

RESEARCH SAYS

❝Different styles of learning suit different children. Some children respond best to sitting down and working with pencils and paper; others prefer physical activity, exploring the world of space, size and shape with their bodies.❞

patterns and sequences

5·00   6·00

Understanding patterns and sequences is fun for your child and helps him to make sense of the world.

Patterns are all around us, from those in the natural world, such as the markings on a zebra, to the patterns in the man-made world, such as road markings, brickwork or the decorative patterns used in art and design. These activities will help your child to identify some of them.

which colour next?

from 3 years

Teach your child about simple alternating patterns using toy bricks.

- Gather a selection of same-sized bricks in two different colours, for example, red and yellow.

- Start a row of red bricks then ask your child to finish the row by adding more red bricks. Do the same with a row of yellow bricks.

- Now make a row using alternating yellow and red bricks. Say the names of the colours as you lay them down, 'red, yellow, red, yellow', and so on.

- Give your child a red and a yellow brick and ask him to choose which one he thinks should go next. If he finds this easy, let him finish the row.

RESEARCH SAYS

‘ Children find it hard to understand that sometimes activities or objects need to follow on after each other in an ordered way. Sequences of two things, such as two differently coloured bricks, are a good introduction to this idea. ’

fingerprint rows
from 3 years

This simple painting exercise is a great way to introduce your child to the concept of pattern.

- Choose three different colours of children's paint.
- Dip your child's finger into one colour and help him to make a row of fingerprints.
- Wipe his finger and let him dip it in the second colour. Make a second row of fingerprints.
- Make a third row of fingerprints with the third colour.
- Make a fourth row of fingerprints with the first colour. Keep repeating the rows of fingerprints until the whole page is filled to make a pattern.

colour squares
from 3 years

Show your child how to create a diagonal pattern of colour using a square grid.

- Draw a grid consisting of 16 squares (four down and four across).
- Select four coloured pencils and colour each square in the top row a different colour, for example, yellow, red, blue and green.
- Colour in the second row of squares, but this time move each colour along one square, for example, green, yellow, red, blue.
- Do the same with the next two rows, moving the colours along one square each time.
- Show your child the diagonal patterns of colour that you've made.

repeating shapes
from 4 years

Can your child guess which shape comes next in the sequence?

- Draw an alternating pattern of two shapes, such as a circle and a rectangle. Say the names of the shapes as you draw them.
- Stop just before you get to a rectangle and ask your child if he can guess which shape you are going to draw next.
- If he finds this difficult, go through the row again pointing out the pattern.
- If he finds this easy, let him finish drawing the row.
- Make the pattern more complex by using three shapes.

animal patterns
from 4 years

Making a chart of animal spots and stripes enhances your child's awareness of patterns in nature.

- Draw two columns on a large piece of paper. One is for spots and one is for stripes.
- In the spots column draw or ask your child to stick in pictures of creatures that have spots, such as a ladybird, leopard, jaguar or butterfly.
- In the stripes column draw or stick in pictures of creatures that have stripes, such as a tiger, bee, wasp, caterpillar or zebra.
- Which column has the most animals?
- Talk about other patterns and markings that you see on animals and insects.

print magic

from 3 years

Making potato prints is a fun and traditional way to learn about shape and pattern.

- Cut a potato in half and sculpt a raised square on one half and a raised triangle on the other. Alternatively, cut cross-sections of a carrot.

- Help your child to dip the potato square into some thick paint, then press it down on the top left-hand corner of the paper. Repeat the print across the top of the paper.

- Dip the potato triangle into a different colour and make a row of triangles underneath the squares.

- Continue alternating rows of squares and triangles until your child has covered the paper.

RESEARCH SAYS

❝ Children classify objects on the basis of a single feature. When introducing the idea of sequences to a child, it's a good idea to present sequences in which only one feature varies, such as shape, colour or size. ❞

build with counters
from 4½ years

How many patterns can your child make from six counters?

- Lay six counters in a row and count them together with your child.

- Rearrange the counters in two rows of three. Count them again.

- Now make the counters into a tower and count them.

- Finally, make a pyramid with three counters in the bottom row, two in the middle and one on top. Count them again.

- Repeat this exercise with different numbers of counters. Which numbers make even rows? Which make pyramids? Which numbers will do both? How many counters do you need to make a square?

RESEARCH SAYS

❜ Counting is not a skill exclusive to humans; animals count too. If lions hear the roar of one lion, they go out to face the enemy, but if they hear three different lions roaring they lie low. ❜

how many legs?
from 4 years

This animal-naming game helps your child to understand that legs come in pairs.

- Ask your child to name creatures that have two legs, for example, a bird, duck, monkey or person.
- Ask him to think of four-legged creatures, for example, a cow, horse, cat or dog.
- Ask him to think of six-legged creatures, for example, a beetle, ladybird, grasshopper or bee.
- Ask him to think of eight-legged creatures, for example, a spider or octopus.
- Point out that all the animals he has named have pairs of legs. Ask him which creature has too many legs to count. A centipede!

one to one hundred
from 4½ years

A hundred-square grid is useful for recognizing many different sorts of number patterns.

- Draw a grid of ten squares by ten squares. Ask your child to make each row a different colour.
- Starting from the top left, write the numbers one to ten along the top row.
- On the second row write the numbers 11 to 20. And so on up to one hundred.
- Point out how each new group of ten starts on a new line and how numbers form patterns. Ask him to draw a line through all the numbers with zero or five in.
- Make this grid on a computer so that you can print out several copies. Use them for colouring in different patterns, such as multiplication tables.

adding on one
from 4 years

This activity is a first introduction to simple addition.

- When your child can count up to ten ask him if he can tell you 'what's one more than one?'.
- If he can, keep going up: 'what's one more than two?', 'what's one more than three?', and so on. Demonstrate with real objects.
- When he's confident, pick numbers under ten at random.
- Eventually, move on to numbers up to 20. Once they grasp the general idea, older children will be able to manage quite large numbers.

making ten
from 4½ years

Teaching your child which pairs of numbers add up to ten is a vital first maths skill.

- Count out ten counters or buttons with your child.
- Lay them in a row then move one counter to the side. Show your child that the one counter plus the nine counters still make ten. Let him count them to make sure and then repeat the exercise himself.
- Lay the counters in a row of ten and move two to the side. Show your child that the two counters plus the eight counters still make ten.
- Repeat with three and seven, four and six, and five and five counters.

missing numbers

from 4½ years

Spotting the
missing number
in a sequence is
often harder than
it seems.

- Write a row of numbers from one to ten, but leave one number out. Read the numbers aloud and ask your child if he can name the missing one.

- If he finds this difficult, draw several rows of oranges, starting with one orange at the top, then two underneath, then three and so on. Miss out a row and ask him if he can guess how many oranges should be in it.

- Throw a ball back and forth – you count odd numbers and your child counts even numbers. Tell your child to shout if you miss out one of your numbers.

- Older children can spot missing numbers in more complicated sequences such as: 10, 20, 30, ..., 50 or 5, 10, 15, ..., 25, ...

RESEARCH SAYS

❛ A child will perceive two evenly spaced rows of counters as containing the same amount, even if they don't. This is because he doesn't yet understand the principle of numerical equality and relies instead on visual impressions. ❜

hands up!
from 3 years

Use the five fingers on your child's hand to practise counting in fives.

- Mix up some runny paint.
- Show your child how to dip her hand in paint and press it down firmly as many times as she can on a large sheet of paper.
- Let the paint dry, then write the numbers one to five across the fingers of each hand print.
- For older children, use your hand poster to talk about the idea of counting in fives, for example, two hands have ten fingers, three hands have fifteen fingers, and so on.

animal ark
from 3 years

Putting pairs of model animals into an ark gives your child a practical understanding of what it means to count in twos.

- Gather some model animals and show your child how to pair them up.
- Ask your child to create a line of paired-up animals.
- Improvise an ark from a large upturned hat or box and count the animals in, saying 'two elephants, two giraffes, two zebras', and so on.
- An older child could count the animals in twos: 'two, four, six, eight, ten', and so on.

at the toy shop

from 3 years

Playing shops
is an excellent
introduction to
counting with
money.

- Help your child set up a pretend shop with five sections. You could put dolls in one, teddies in the second, bricks in the third and so on.
- Give your child some toy money. Stick to one type of coin of low value.
- Make labels to show how much each toy costs. Write the price and draw the corresponding number of coins next to it.
- Ask her to choose which toy she would like to buy, and help her to count out the number of coins she needs.
- Now it's your child's turn to be the shopkeeper while you choose a toy to buy.

RESEARCH SAYS

6 **Playing counting games and doing simple sums with your child increases her confidence and shows her that numbers are fun. If she is reluctant to learn about numbers don't push her – you can always try again another time.** 9

watch the clock!

from 4½ years

A child who is confident with numbers up to 12 may be ready to start telling the time.

- Using a paper plate, draw a large clock face with the numbers clearly marked around the edge. Cut out card hands for the clock and attach them to the face with a paper fastener. Alternatively, use a toy clock.

- Put the big hand to 12 o'clock, then gradually move the small hand around the clock face telling your child the time at each new number.

- Now move the small hand to various numbers at random and ask your child if he can guess what time it is.

- Talk about things you might do at different times of the day, for instance at 1 o'clock you have lunch; at 6 o'clock you have dinner; at 7 o'clock you have a bath; and at 8 o'clock you're fast asleep!

RESEARCH SAYS

❝ Whereas adults perceive time in a linear way, children tend to live in the present. It isn't until he reaches the age of three, that your child begins to understand the concept of today, yesterday and tomorrow. ❞

which goes where?
from 4 years

Help your child to understand the cycle of day and night.

- Set out two large sheets of paper. Tell your child that one sheet is for day and the other is for night.

- Name various things associated with either day or night, such as sun, breakfast, bicycle, or moon, bed, pyjamas. Ask your child whether each thing belongs to day or night and draw it on the appropriate sheet.

- When both sheets are full, put them up on your child's wall to remind him of the difference between day and night.

how long will it take?
from 4½ years

Timing how long he spends on different activities helps your child to understand the passage of time.

- Using a home-made clock face (see Watch the clock!) or a toy clock, help your child to count the number of hours he spends doing everyday activities.

- Start by looking at morning activities. If your child spends an hour at playgroup, show him where the clock hands start and finish for this activity.

- Now look at the duration of afternoon activities together. Try to choose activities that last for differing numbers of hours.

- An older child can make a simple chart on squared paper to show how long activities take, using one square for every hour. Discuss which activity takes longest and which is the quickest.

sorting and matching

Sorting objects into groups that share similar characteristics requires careful thinking.

Arranging shapes, putting things in pairs or matching up identical pictures can provide a good foundation for future reading skills. These challenging yet enjoyable activities help improve your child's observational skills and develop his memory.

fruity fun
from 3 years

Sorting fruit into categories of type, colour and shape encourages your child to be aware of different characteristics of familiar objects.

- Put a selection of fruit of different colours and shapes on the table.

- Hold up a banana and ask your child to find you another one. Do the same with the other fruit on the table. Ask your child to name each fruit and say what colour it is.

- Now ask your child to sort the fruit by colour. For example, yellow fruit, such as bananas, lemons and grapefruit, and red fruit, such as strawberries, cherries and red apples.

- Finally, sort the fruit by shape, for example, long fruit such as bananas, and round fruit, such as oranges. You can also sort fruit according to whether it is soft, such as peaches, or hard, such as apples.

where do we live?
from 3 years

This sorting game helps your child to identify animal names and types.

- Put some toy animals on the table.

- Tell your child that one corner of the table is the jungle, another is the farm, another is the sea and the last is the dinosaur swamp. Vary the categories to suit the animals.

- Hold one animal up and say, 'This is a pig. Do you think he lives in the jungle, farm, sea or dinosaur swamp?'

- If your child answers correctly, let him put the animal in the right corner. If not, give him a clue to work it out.

- Do the same with the other animals.

the big toy sort!

from 3 years

A toybox tidy-up can easily be turned into a first sorting game.

- Tip a box of muddled-up toys on to the floor.
- Ask your child to search for one category of toy, for example, play figures, while you look for another, for example, jigsaw pieces.
- When you've both found as many items as you can, put them into their own containers. Start a new search for other categories of toy.
- When all the toys are sorted, ask your child to count how many categories you found. Your child can also divide his toys into sub-categories, for example, vehicles can be sorted into cars, lorries and buses.

RESEARCH SAYS

❝ When learning about classifying objects, your child needs to understand that an object can be grouped in more than one way. For example, an orange can belong to a group of orange objects, spherical objects or a group of fruit. ❞

what's it worth?
from 4½ years

Help your child understand how coins relate to each other by compiling this chart.

- At the top of a piece of paper draw a picture of the lowest-value coin.

- Draw a vertical line down the centre of the paper.

- To the left of the line, draw a picture of the second-lowest-value coin. To the right, draw its equivalent in lowest-value coins.

- Continue like this, with coins rising in value down the left, and equivalent low-value amounts on the right. Don't go too high or it will become confusing.

my money box
from 4½ years

Counting your savings is a very personal way to become familiar with sorting out money!

- Give your child a money box or make one from a small box with a slit cut in the top.

- Give your child some coins and show her how to post them in the slot. Let her feel how the box gets heavier each time more coins are added.

- Add coins regularly over a few days or weeks. When the box is nearly full, let your child open it up and sort all the coins into piles.

- Help your child count up how much each pile is worth, then add them together for the grand total.

rub a coin

from 4 years

Rubbing coins encourages your child to observe patterns and helps her to identify different coins.

- Give your child some coins. Ask your child if she knows the names of any of them. If she doesn't, tell her.

- Ask her to sort the coins into matching groups. Point out that the size of the coin doesn't necessarily indicate its value.

- Choose a coin and place it under a sheet of plain paper.

- Give your child a crayon and tell her to rub firmly on the coin through the paper. As the pattern of the coin emerges, ask her which coin it is.

- When your child has done several coin rubbings, help her to cut them out and line them up beside the real coins, saying their names as you do so.

RESEARCH SAYS

❛ Playing games with coins provides children with a basic understanding of the sequence of numbers. This is especially true if they use coins to buy treats, as a coin of greater numerical value than another can be used to buy more treats! ❜

spot the twins

from 3 years

Teach your child to use colour coding to match items.

- Draw three stick girls with triangular skirts and four stick boys wearing shorts.

- Colour each girl's skirt a different colour and three of the boys' shorts in matching colours. Colour the fourth boy's shorts in a completely different colour.

- Ask your child to spot the 'twins' – the stick figures with matching colour clothes.

- Can she point out which stick figure isn't part of a twin?

RESEARCH SAYS

❛ For your child to learn to count properly she needs to match a word, such as 'three', with a quantity, such as three balloons. Games that teach general matching skills develop your child's ability to make associations. ❜

dolly's wardrobe
from 3 years

Matching clothes to toys involves comparing sizes, and dressing them requires your child to follow a logical order.

- Choose two or three dolls or teddies of significantly different sizes.
- Find one or more outfits, including socks and/or shoes, to fit each toy.
- Put all the clothes in one pile and the toys in another.
- Ask your child if she can sort out which clothes fit which toy. Now help her to dress her toys. Show her how to put clothes on in the right order, for example, a dress before a coat, and socks before shoes.

pick a shape
from 3 years

Play this game with your child to encourage shape identification and sorting.

- From card, cut out some circles, squares, triangles, rectangles, stars, diamonds and ovals. Cut out the same number of each shape.
- Lay a row of different shapes on the floor. Put the rest in a bag or envelope.
- Ask your child to take a shape out of the envelope and place it beneath its matching one on the floor.
- Now it's your turn. If you pick a shape that's already been put down, replace it in the envelope; if not, lay it on the floor.
- The first person to complete a whole row wins that round. Repeat with another row. Continue until all the shapes are used up.

funny socks

from 3 years

This matching game is similar to Pairs (see page 84) but is fun and easier for younger children.

- Cut out 14 sock outlines from card and arrange them into seven pairs.
- Using a selection of art materials, such as sticky dots, sequins, gold stars, tissue paper and crayons, help your child to decorate each pair of socks in a distinctive way.
- Put all the finished socks face down on a table. Take turns to turn over two socks. If they match, keep them and have another go. If they don't, turn them back over.
- The person with the most sock pairs is the winner.

match the cup

from 4 years

This exercise helps your child to match items using colour and shades of colour.

- Take a piece of paper and draw five different colour cups at the top.
- At the bottom of the paper draw five stick girls with triangular skirts. Colour the skirts in the same five colours, or similar shades, such as lilac and purple, as the cups.
- Ask your child to draw a line that joins each cup to the girl with the same colour skirt.
- Repeat the game but add an extra girl and ask your child if she can spot which girl hasn't got a cup. Can your child draw and colour a cup for her?

muddle and match

from 3 years

Children enjoy fitting boxes, cups and saucepans back together again, and they learn to match shapes in the process.

- Gather several two-piece items, such as storage boxes and lids, a plastic bottle and cap, a saucepan and lid, a drinking beaker and top, or the top and bottom of a soap dish.

- Separate all the tops from the bottoms and muddle them all up on the floor.

- Ask your child to match the pieces that fit together.

RESEARCH SAYS

❛ It is much easier for your child to point out two objects that are identical to one another than match up items that don't resemble each other in size, shape or colour. For example, a hat and a scarf. ❜

copy my colours
from 4½ years

It's quite a challenge to copy accurately but this exercise quickly hones your child's counting and observation skills.

- Draw two grids consisting of 16 squares (four down and four across) each.

- Colour a selection of squares at random on the first grid.

- Ask your child to colour in exactly the same squares on the second grid.

- If she finds this difficult, suggest she looks closely at each row in turn. Put a ruler under each row to guide her eye.

RESEARCH SAYS

❛ The ability to notice differences and similarities between objects is a very useful pre-reading skill. If your child is adept at noticing fine details, it will help her to recognize words when she starts learning to read. ❜

identical faces
from 3 years

This activity encourages your child to notice small but significant details in pictures.

- Draw six oval shapes on a piece of paper.
- Make two ovals into identical faces with glasses, a hat and a beard (for example). Make the remaining four ovals into faces that differ from the first two in subtle but important details, such as no beard, or without glasses.
- Show the faces to your child and ask her if she can spot which two faces are exactly the same.
- Vary this game by making the facial details easier or harder to spot.

find my partner
from 4 years

This matching game helps your child to apply the everyday observations he has made about the world around him.

- Take a large piece of paper and fold it down the middle.
- On the left, draw one item from a pair of objects that you might expect to go together, for example, a bowl and spoon, hat and scarf, chair and table or chicken and egg. On the right, lower down, draw the other item of the pair.
- Continue like this with other sets of pairs.
- Ask your child if he can draw a line linking each pair.

snap!
from 4 years

This favourite game is great for improving number recognition skills.

- Shuffle a pack of playing cards and deal it into two halves. Give your child one half and keep the other.
- Put your cards, face down, in front of you. Take turns to turn over your top card and place it, face up, in a new pile in the centre. If it matches the one immediately below it shout 'snap!'.
- The person who shouts 'snap!' first keeps all the cards in the centre pile and adds them, face down, to the bottom of his own pile.
- The first person to collect the whole pack wins.
- A younger child could play this game with a pack of 'snap' picture cards.

pairs
from 4½ years

This card-matching game not only helps your child to recognize numbers, but also improves his memory.

- Shuffle a pack of playing cards and lay each one face down.
- Tell your child to turn over two cards. If they match, he can keep the pair and have another go. If they don't, he must turn them back over in their original position.
- Now it's your turn to do the same.
- Continue like this until all the cards have gone. The winner is the person who has collected the most pairs.
- To make it easier, put out only five or ten pairs of cards.

red or black?

from 3 years

Playing card games is an excellent way to learn about matching and sorting items in different ways, and children love playing with grown-up 'toys'.

- Start by sorting a pack of playing cards into two piles: red cards and black cards.

- Now show your child how he can divide the red pile again into hearts and diamonds, and the black pile into clubs or spades.

- Ask him to find the picture cards in all of the piles.

- An older child will enjoy helping you put the suits in rising numerical order, or sorting out groups of four matching numbers.

RESEARCH SAYS

❛ As your child's cognitive skills become increasingly sophisticated, he will be able to sort playing cards in an increasing number of ways. At first by colour and then, over time, his sorting ability will extend to number, suit and picture cards as well. ❜

guess ahead

Your child needs to absorb huge amounts of information in his everyday life.

It's not always easy to filter out what's important and what can safely be ignored. These games all give your child practice in resolving situations that require logical decisions. Most involve active discussion, so allow enough time to talk through the game together.

bobbing along
from 3 years

Predicting what will float and what will sink helps your child to make observations about different objects.

- Fill a sink or bowl with water.
- Ask your child to help you choose a number of household objects, for example, a cork, a sponge, a plastic beaker, a toy boat, a teaspoon, a wooden spoon, a sieve, an apple and a pebble.
- Before dropping each one in the water, ask your child to guess whether it will sink or float and why.

RESEARCH SAYS

❝ Children, like adults, base their predictions on practical experience. For example, if every time your child presses a button on a toy, a nursery rhyme plays, he will learn to predict that pressing that button triggers the rhyme. ❞

how far can you go?
from 4 years

Making a sensible estimate is a very useful pre-maths skill.

- Ask your child to stand at a starting line, and guess how far he can throw a small soft ball.

- Mark the spot he thinks he can reach, then ask him to throw the ball, and see how close he gets.

- If his original guess was very inaccurate, ask him to guess again, and mark a new spot before getting him to take another throw.

- Other ideas for your child to guess about: how far he can roll a ball along the ground; how far he can hop without putting down his second foot; and how many times you can throw and catch a ball between you without dropping it.

make them grow
from 4½ years

This game offers lots of counting practice and encourages your child to predict what will happen next.

- Draw a simple picture of a tree with five nuts on it. Ask your child to count the nuts.

- Below, draw the same tree with the nuts on the ground beneath it – your child may like to write the numbers by each one if you write them faintly for him first.

- Ask your child what he thinks may happen to the nuts now that they're on the ground.

- A third picture can show the nuts now growing into five little trees growing up in front of the big tree.

- If your child enjoys this game, he could add five little nuts to each of the new young trees.

freeze frame!

from 4 years

This experiment shows your child how water expands when it freezes.

- Explain to your child that you can heat up water by boiling it in a kettle, or make it cold by putting it in the fridge or freezer.

- Find a clear plastic beaker and half fill it with water, marking the level of the water on the outside.

- Put it in the freezer. Ask your child what she thinks might happen to it if it stays in there all night.

- The next morning, show your child how the ice has 'grown' by comparing the level of the ice to the original mark on the beaker. Mark the new level. Can she guess what will happen to the level if you leave the water to defrost?

- You can try this experiment using fruit juice so that your child learns how ice-lollies are made.

a sticky situation

from 3 years

Making a sticky dough is a great way to learn about what can happen when you mix a solid with a liquid.

- Give your child a large bowl containing several tablespoons of flour.

- Encourage your child to run his fingers through the flour. Talk about how soft and dry the flour feels.

- Give her a small cup of water and ask what will happen if she adds it to the flour. Now let her find out. Add the water a little at a time and keep stirring.

- Can she describe what is happening? Point out that flour and water mixed together form a totally new substance.

- When the consistency is right for kneading, help your child to roll it out or add salt to make modelling dough.

- Try the same experiment but starting with water and adding flour gradually. Can your child guess the result?

all mixed up

from 4 years

Give your child a first lesson about what happens when you mix two colours together to make a new one.

- Put some red, yellow, blue and white paint on a palette and give your child an old plate to mix colours on.

- Ask your child to guess what colour she will make if she mixes red and yellow, blue and yellow or white and red. Now let her mix them to find out.

- Experiment by mixing different proportions of the colours, for example, using a tiny amount of red with lots of white.

- Help your child make a chart to show how colours mix to make other ones, for example, red + yellow = orange.

- Talk about colour mixes in everyday life. For example, make a cup of black coffee and ask your child what will happen to the colour if you add milk.

RESEARCH SAYS

6 Young children do not think in the same way that adults do. If something changes its appearance, a child will believe that it has changed permanently, for example, water changing into ice. They will not realize that it can become water again. 9

mind the gap

from 4 years

Encourage your child to think about the meaning and context of words in this sentence-building exercise.

- Describe a scene to your child, such as, 'It's a wet day and the rain is pouring down'.
- Miss out a word from the next sentence and ask your child to guess what that word might be. For example, 'I must remember to put up my ... '.
- Continue in the same way. For example, 'If I put up my umbrella, I will stay nice and ... '.
- Vary the game with sentences describing everyday activities, such as, 'I wash my hair with ... ', or 'I like to ride my ... in the park'.

what should we do?

from 3 years

This exercise demonstrates to your child that considering consequences in everyday life can help to prevent problems.

- Ask your child the following questions. If she gets the answer right, ask her how she could have prevented the outcome.
- What happens if you don't have a drink all day?
- What happens if you don't dry yourself when you get out of the bath?
- What happens if you leave a cake too long in the oven?
- What happens if you forget to fill the car with petrol?

the deepest puddle

from 4 years

This puddle tour helps your child to develop practical problem-solving and measuring skills.

- Go for a walk with your child after it's been raining. Take a ruler with you or find a stick.

- Talk about how puddles gather in dips in the ground. Ask your child if she can predict which of several puddles is the deepest.

- Ask her to dip her ruler or stick into a puddle. How far does the water come up the ruler in terms of finger-widths?

- Use the ruler or stick to measure the other puddles. Did she guess the deepest one correctly?

RESEARCH SAYS

‘ **By monitoring brain activity using scanning equipment, scientists have been able to determine that specific parts of the brain are involved in certain tasks. When people are asked to judge whether one number is bigger than another, a specific area of the brain lights up.** ’

weather report

from 4 years

Watching the
weather together
teaches your child
prediction skills
and helps him to
plan ahead.

- Each morning look out of the window and ask your child to describe the sky and the weather.
- Can he suggest what might happen later? For example, will it be rainy or sunny?
- What clothes does your child think he should wear? Will he need a change of clothes later?
- Draw simple pictures of the weather on a week-long weather chart.

RESEARCH SAYS

❝ Your child may be able to make simple predictions, for example, if he drops a glass, it will smash. Complex predictions, in which A doesn't always lead to B, may pose more of a challenge. ❞

how many shoes?
from 3 years

This drawing game helps to extend your child's counting ability.

- Draw a picture of a little boy. Ask your child how many shoes the boy needs. Ask him to draw on the shoes.
- Draw a cat. If the cat wore shoes, how many would she need? Ask your child to draw shoes on.
- Do the same with an ant and then a caterpillar (with as many legs as your child can count).

how would I feel?
from 4½ years

This activity encourages your child to think about which emotions are appropriate to which situations.

- Set the scene for several situations that would provoke a strong emotion. For example, 'I'm sitting on a beach in the sunshine with a nice cool drink'. Or, 'I'm standing at a bus stop in the rain and I'm very hungry'.
- Give your children a list of emotions, such as happy, sad, angry or frightened, and ask him which he would feel in each situation.
- Ask your child to make up his own situations that would provoke these feelings.

I've had a letter
from 3 years

This exercise shows your child how to use picture clues to deduce the meaning of a sentence.

- Write a simple letter to your child, describing a few events of the day.

- In each sentence, replace one of the words with a picture clue. For example, 'Then I sat down and read my ... '.

- Read each sentence to your child and see if he can supply the missing word. If not, point the picture clue out to him.

picture treasure hunt
from 4 years

All children love treasure hunts and they learn about following clues in the process.

- Cut out five pieces of card and number them one to five. On the reverse side draw a picture clue, such as a bath, sofa, bed, toy box and chair. Hide the cards around the house in numerical order so that each card leads your child to the location of the next card.

- For younger children, make sure the clue cards are clearly visible in each location.

- Hide a prize in the location shown on the fifth card.

- Send your child on a treasure hunt. Once he has found the prize, lay all five cards out in number order and count them together.

what happens if ... ?

from 3 years

Encourage your child to make logical deductions about what might happen next in a series of practical situations.

- Stand at the sink and let water flow into a bowl. Ask your child what will happen when the water reaches the top of the bowl. What about if you left the plug in the sink?

- Build a tower of bricks and wait until you think it might fall. Ask your child what he thinks will happen if you add one more brick.

- Build a tower of rectangular wooden bricks (stacked in alternate directions in rows of three). Ask your child to remove one brick at a time. In each case ask him what the effect will be.

RESEARCH SAYS

❛ **By the age of four, your child is able to search systematically for a single object, but if he is asked to find several objects he will look for them strictly in the order that they are presented to him.** ❜

fill in the story

from 4½ years

This game promotes your child's memory and also makes him think about story structure.

- Start telling your child a familiar story.
- When you reach an exciting part of the story, pause and let your child tell you what happens next.
- Your child may find this easier if you choose a story that contains a rhyme or a familiar refrain.
- If he's confident, let him tell the story to you, gently prompting him if he gets stuck.

RESEARCH SAYS

6 The intelligence of a child at the age of three is not a good predictor of adult intelligence. Measured at the age of four, however, a reliable indication can be given of intelligence later in life. 9

story scramble
from 4 years

This enjoyable game teaches your child to construct a logical narrative.

- Divide a piece of paper into four sections.
- Draw part of a story on each section. For example, a girl walks along; it starts to rain; she puts up her umbrella; she sees a rainbow.
- Cut the pictures out and put them in the wrong order. Ask your child to put them back in the correct sequence and tell you the story.
- If he finds this difficult, give him a head start by telling him the story first.

how can I escape?
from 4½ years

Build your child's imagination and story-telling ability by asking him to think about escaping from fantasy scenarios.

- Tell your child that he is swimming underwater with a net and a torch when he bumps into a big hungry shark. Ask your child what he would do. Suggest how he might escape.
- Invent other fantasy scenarios. For example, your child is armed only with a balloon, a sandwich and a bottle of water and he is being chased by a lion in the jungle or a snake in the desert.

what's wrong?

Children get huge satisfaction and a boost to their confidence when they get things right.

You can have lots of fun by setting up situations where there's a deliberate mistake for your child to identify and correct. The games in this chapter include visual as well as verbal activities that will help your child exercise her powers of logical thinking. And you can laugh about the silly scenarios you create together.

what's in the way?

from 4 years

This imaginary road trip helps your child to come up with his own solutions to practical problems.

- Draw a wiggly road on a large piece of paper, making the road wide enough for a toy car. Draw a house at the end of the road.

- Ask your child to suggest possible hold-ups that could stop the car getting to the house. For example, a fallen tree, a ditch, a flood or a cow standing in the road.

- Draw each of these obstacles on the road.

- Ask your child to push his toy car along the road. As he encounters each obstacle, ask him how he is going to overcome it. If he finds this difficult, suggest your own solutions, such as chopping up the fallen tree, filling in the ditch or hooting the car horn at the cow.

RESEARCH SAYS

❛ Tasks that involve spotting absurdities in pictures, answering questions about how to overcome obstacles, and spotting the odd-one-out in a sequence of items all help to cultivate verbal reasoning. ❜

mind the cars
from 3 years

This fun game helps your child to apply his practical knowledge of transport and how things move.

- Draw some simple outlines of vehicles, missing out an important part in each case. For example, a car or train without wheels, or a plane with a wing missing.
- Ask your child to spot the missing part.
- Draw in the missing part but make it wrong. For example, draw square wheels on a car, or feet on a train.
- Ask your child if he can spot anything wrong. Would the vehicle be able to move?

odd one out
from 4 years

All children enjoy spotting the odd one out and it builds their ability to reason.

- Say a list of words that contains one odd one. For example, 'car, boat, plane, train, egg', or 'cat, dog, horse, glove, sheep'. Ask your child to identify the odd one out.
- If he finds this difficult, give him a clue, or pause just before you say the odd word.
- An older child may enjoy coming up with his own lists, or drawing pictures of the items.

getting around
from 4 years

Teach your child to apply his knowledge about animals and the way they move.

- Talk about the different ways that people and animals move around, such as running, walking and swimming. Ask your child the following questions (or make up your own).

- Which creature is best at flying: a butterfly or an elephant? Easy questions like this will help your child to get the idea of the game.

- Which creature is best at slithering along the ground: a snake or a bear?

- Which creature is best at swimming: a fish or a bird?

- Which creature is best at climbing: a monkey or a dog?

whose house?
from 4 years

This game helps your child to make reasoned judgements about which creatures live where – and why.

- Describe the home of a particular creature and ask your child who he thinks might live there.

- For example, a nest high up in a tree made from twigs and leaves.

- Help your child by giving him a choice of creatures, for example, a dog, a bird or an elephant.

- Talk about how silly it would be, for example, for an elephant or a dog to live in a nest in a tree.

- Ask your child to draw a picture of the correct creature in its home.

animal crackers

from 4 years

Children enjoy the silliness of these mixed-up animals and it gives you an opportunity to talk about how an animal's body is adapted to its environment.

- Choose three animals, and talk with your child about their most obvious characteristics, such as a snake with its long, scaly body; a pig with its snout and curly tail, and a hedgehog with its prickly spines.

- Draw one of the animals but add a wrong characteristic, for example, a snake with hedgehog spines.

- Ask your child to spot what's wrong and to describe what the animal should look like.

- Ask him to draw an accurate picture of the animal.

RESEARCH SAYS

6 An adult will apply the rules of logic to any given situation but a preschool child will believe what he sees. This is why children find illogical pictures, such as a cat with a bird's wings, very funny. 9

what's missing?

from 3 years

This drawing game encourages your child to think about the appearance and function of everyday objects.

- Draw a picture of a household item with an important bit missing, for example, a table with only three legs or a teapot without a spout.

- Ask your child what's missing from the picture.

- If she notices straight away, ask her to draw in the missing item.

- If she finds it difficult, offer clues such as, 'Look at each corner of the table'.

- Talk about what would happen to a real table if it only had three legs.

RESEARCH SAYS

❝ When information enters memory, it may be encoded visually (as a mental picture) or acoustically (as sound). Information such as the layout of a familiar room is encoded visually, whereas a nursery rhyme is encoded acoustically. ❞

crazy story
from 4 years

Test your child's memory of familiar stories and encourage her to spot mistakes.

- Start telling a familiar story to your child. Ask your child to stop you if she hears anything wrong.
- Introduce a detail that deviates from the usual story, for example, Little Red Riding Hood meeting a cow instead of a wolf on the way to her grandmother's house.
- Ask your child to correct you. Let her continue the story if she wants to.

which room?
from 4 years

This game helps your child to visualize familiar spaces and make reasoned decisions.

- Tell your child that you're going to describe one of the rooms in your house and to shout out 'stop!' if she hears anything wrong.
- Start with an accurate description of your bathroom, for example, and then introduce an anomaly, such as a bed next to the bath or a cooker in the corner.
- If she finds this hard, stop and question her by saying, for example, 'A cooker in the bathroom! Is that right?'.

true or false?

from 4 years

This game teaches your child to differentiate between a true statement and a false one.

- Explain the concepts of true and false to your child and ask him to apply them to the following statements.
- 'Fish like walking along the pavement.'
- 'Monkeys can swing through the trees.'
- 'The sea is pink.'
- You can also use this game to reinforce safety messages, such as, 'It is dangerous to run out in the road without looking'.

my busy day

from 4½ years

Untangling a mixed-up sentence exercises your child's problem-solving skills.

- Talk about the activities you and your child do regularly each day.
- Tell him you're going to mix up two words in a sentence. For example, 'We're going to the ducks to feed the park'. Or, 'Let's go and hair your brush'. Ask him if he can tell you which words have been swapped.
- If he enjoys this, muddle the words even more. For example, 'that squirrel jumping look at!'.

sing-song
from 4 years

Children love nursery rhymes and delight in correcting your deliberate mistakes.

- Start singing a familiar nursery rhyme or song to your child. Ask your child to stop and tell you if he hears anything wrong.

- Introduce a mistake, such as 'Jack and Jill went up the hill to fetch a pail of milk'.

- Ask your child for the correct word or phrase and let him continue to the end if he wants to.

RESEARCH SAYS

6 Children are getting cleverer year by year. The average IQ in the UK has risen by 27 points since 1942. Research suggests similar improvements in other European countries, the US and Japan. 9

spot the difference
from 4 years

This game helps your child to look closely at the details in pictures and to see beyond the obvious similarities.

- Draw simple but identical pictures side by side, such as two fish, two cups and saucers, and two dolls.

- Make two or three minor adjustments to one of each pair, for example, adding some spots and an extra fin to one of the fish.

- Ask your child to look at the two pictures and tell you what are the differences between them.

- If she finds this difficult, offer clues, such as, 'look at the tail'.

- Your child may enjoy adding her own 'differences' to a set of pictures.

RESEARCH SAYS

❛ Concepts simplify and order the world by dividing it into manageable units. Children learn that the concept of an object includes certain properties. They then apply this concept to that 'type' of object, regardless of size, colour or shape. ❜

all dressed up
from 3 years

Sorting her clothes is a practical way for your child to learn about the usefulness of putting things in a logical order.

- Gather some clothes that you would like your child to wear. Ask her to arrange them in the order in which she will put them on.

- Now pretend to put all her clothes on the wrong parts of her body. For example, her trousers on her head and her socks on her hands.

- Ask her if anything is wrong and, if so, to tell you the correct part of her body for each item of clothing.

why doesn't it work?
from 4½ years

These fantasy scenarios will not only make your child laugh, they'll teach her to apply the practical knowledge that she's learned about the world.

- Draw a series of silly scenes and ask your child to spot what is wrong in each case. Can she redraw the scene correctly?

- A man with an umbrella in which the rain is falling underneath the umbrella instead of on top of it.

- A plant growing upside down with its roots in the air and the flower underground.

- A woman wearing glasses on the back of her head.

- A clock with the numbers in the wrong order.

- A sky with stars and a sun.

- A snowman on a sunny beach.

musical games

Pre-school children respond instinctively to nursery rhymes, songs and music.

Children's natural love of music means that it is a great aid to learning. Try these ideas for counting songs, first music-and-movement activities and rhythm and melody games. Listening to music together at any time will provide stimulation and enjoyment.

hammer 'n' count!

from 3 years

The physical actions in this counting rhyme will help your child to remember the numbers.

- Show your child how to make her right hand into a fist and pretend to hammer with it while singing this song:

  'Peter hammers with one hammer, one hammer, one hammer.
  Peter hammers with one hammer,
  All day long.'

- Ask your child to make her left hand into a fist as well and sing, 'Peter hammers with two hammers ... '.

- Add an extra hammer in each verse until you get to five (your child can stamp her feet and nod her head for the other hammers).

RESEARCH SAYS

❝ **Reading and singing nursery rhymes to your child teaches her not only about rhythm and melody, but also about counting and vocabulary. Children who are read and sung to at home have a head start when they go to school.** ❞

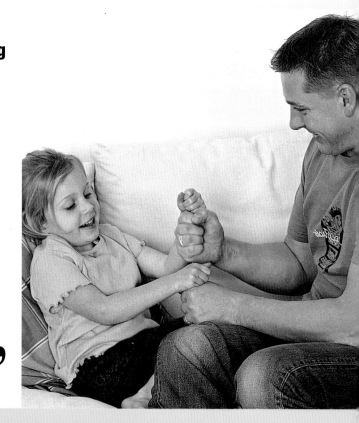

five little ducks
from 3 years

Use this favourite rhyme to help your child practise counting down from five.

- Cut out five duck shapes from a piece of card. Your child can decorate them. Line them up in a row and sing this rhyme, removing one duck when you get to the last line:

  'Five little ducks went swimming one day,
  Over the hills and far away.
  Mummy Duck said "Quack, quack, come back!"
  But only four little ducks swam back.'

- Keep singing the rhyme until there are no more ducks, then make the ducks reappear in the final verse:

  'No little ducks went swimming one day,
  Over the hills and far away.
  Mummy Duck said, "Quack, quack, come back!"
  And all five ducks came swimming right back!'

one, two...
from 4 years

This familiar action rhyme teaches your child to count in twos.

- Act out this rhyme with your child. You can use real props (gather some pencils to use as sticks) or mime the actions.

  'One, two, buckle my shoe.
  Three, four, knock at the door.
  Five, six, pick up sticks.
  Seven, eight, lay them straight.
  Nine, ten, a big fat hen!'

happy song

from 4 years

This adaptation
of the well-known
song turns counting
into a fun activity.

- Act out the following song with your child (the line endings are different from the original version):

  'If you're happy and you know it, clap your hands one time.

  If you're happy and you know it, clap your hands one time.

  If you're happy and you know it, then you surely want to show it,

  If you're happy and you know it, clap your hands one time!'

- In the next three verses change the line endings to, 'wave your arm two times', 'shake your leg three times' and 'nod your head four times'.

RESEARCH SAYS

❛ **Verbal, musical and action memories are stored in three different areas of the brain. This explains why people who experience memory loss and cannot learn a new story may still be able to learn to sing or play a new tune.** ❜

going to the zoo
from 3 years

This game introduces your child to the concept of adding 'one more'.

- Start by singing this rhyme:

  'How many creatures went to the zoo?
  Me and you and one more too.
  It ... was ... a ... horse.
  Neigh, neigh, we heard him say.
  How many went to the zoo that day?'

- Put a toy horse on the table and count to three (you, your child and the horse).

- Now sing the next verse and add a cow. Keep going until you run out of toy animals!

finish that song
from 4 years

The tune and rhythm of this nursery rhyme will prompt your child to remember numbers.

- Sing the following rhyme:

  'One, two, three, four, five,
  Once I caught a fish alive.
  Six, seven, eight, nine, ten,
  Then I put him back again!'

- Sing the song again, pausing to allow your child to say the numbers five and ten.

- If she finds this easy, let her say more of the numbers, or see if she can sing the whole song on her own.

one potato, two potato
from 4 years

This well known playground rhyme gives your child basic counting practice.

- Recite the rhyme below, gently banging one fist on top of the other.

  'One potato, two potato,
  Three potato, four.
  Five potato, six potato,
  Seven potato, more!'

- Make up variations on this rhyme by substituting other three-syllable words for 'potato', such as 'tomato' or 'marshmallow'.

pirate ship
from 4 years

Use this rhyme to teach your child that numbers can reflect a person's age.

- Recite this rhyme and ask your child to act out the captain's lines.

  'When I was one I sucked my thumb
  The day I went to sea. I jumped aboard a pirate ship
  And the captain said to me:
  "We're going this way, that way,
  Forwards and backwards, over the Irish sea.
  A bottle of rum to fill my tum and that's the life for me!" '

- Begin each new verse with a new age. For example:

  'When I was two I buckled my shoe.'
  'When I was three I bumped my knee.'
  'When I was four I opened the door.'
  'When I was five I did a dive.'

five little monkeys

from 3 years

Children love this mischievous song and learn to count down from five as they act it out.

- Find four soft toys and sit them on the floor. Say this rhyme in a bouncy rhythm, inviting your child to join in the actions:

  'Five little monkeys jumping on the bed'
  (bounce up and down)

  'One fell off and bumped his head' (rub your head)

  'We called for the doctor' (pretend to dial)

  'And the doctor said,

  "No more monkeys jumping on the bed!"'
  (wag your finger).

- Take one toy away and repeat the verse with four monkeys. Keep going until you are down to one little monkey (your child) then change the last line to:

  'You're the last little monkey jumping on this bed!'

RESEARCH SAYS

❝A mnemonic is a device to aid memory. Nursery rhymes that include counting up and down serve as important mnemonics for children who are learning to memorize number order.❞

stepping stones
from 4 years

This musical game teaches your child that the bigger your steps, the fewer you need to take to get somewhere.

- Tell your child that he's on a magical riverbank. As long as music is playing he is safe. But when the music stops he must cross the river on stepping stones.

- Play some music that he can dance to.

- Stop the music and tell your child to cross the river on three elephant stepping stones, taking giant-sized steps.

- Next time you stop the music he must cross the river on nine small mouse stepping stones. Count them with him.

- Introduce other numbers and sizes of stepping stones, such as five medium-sized fox stepping stones, six small rabbit stepping stones, four big wolf stepping stones, and ten tiny beetle stepping stones. Finish with 12 just-right-sized people stepping stones!

how many?
from 4½ years

This game challenges both your child's physical and counting skills!

- Choose a rhyme that your child knows the words to, such as Twinkle Twinkle Little Star or Humpty Dumpty.

- Sing the song and ask your child to skip. Can he count the number of skips he can do while you are singing the rhyme?

- Now ask him to count the number of hops, jumps, stamps and claps he can do in one rhyme.

- Make a chart together that shows how many of each activity your child did.

on the march

from 3 years

Marching games give your child a regular rhythm to count along to.

- Play some lively music and march around the room counting up to ten.

- As you get to ten, shout out an action for your child to do. Vary the action each time, for example, jump, hop, sit down, turn around, curl in a ball or stretch up tall.

- Make the game more difficult by stopping at a number between one and ten and asking your child to perform an action that number of times.

- Instead of marching, tell your child he must hop until five, then skip until ten. Your child can beat a toy drum in time to his marching.

RESEARCH SAYS

❝ Marching, jumping and skipping helps children to let off steam and get their blood pumping around their body. Children need this kind of physical exertion if they are to settle down, concentrate and learn effectively. ❞

hunt the brick

from 4 years

This hide-and-seek game encourages your child to be aware of different volumes of sound.

- Hide ten small wooden bricks in a room and ask your child to look for them.

- Tell your child that you will help her to find the bricks by shaking a rattle. The nearer she is to a brick, the louder the noise of the rattle; the further away she is, the softer the noise of the rattle.

- You can extend this game by drawing ten bricks on a piece of paper (write the number beside each one) and getting your child to colour each one in as she finds it.

RESEARCH SAYS

6 A child's awareness of sound can be honed by encouraging her to tune in to the range of sounds in her environment and listen carefully to the subtle differences between sounds. 9

where am I?

from 4 years

Can your child use logic to work out where you are from the sounds you describe?

- Describe these sounds to your child (or try imitating them) and ask her to guess where you might be.

  'I can hear seagulls above my head and water lapping on sand.'

  'I can hear cows mooing, a cock crowing and a tractor rumbling.'

  'I can hear children laughing, presents being opened and balloons popping.'

  'I can hear bicycle bells and ducks quacking.'

- When you next go to any of these places try standing still with your child and listing all the actual sounds you hear.

sound pairs

from 4 years

This game teaches your child to become sensitive to the differences between sounds.

- Collect six identical plastic bottles. Cover the outsides with paper so that the contents can't be seen.

- Put some salt in two of the bottles, some rice in another two and some dried beans in the last two. Replace the caps securely.

- Mix up the bottles and ask your child to shake each one in turn, then put them together in pairs.

- When she's finished, let her remove the paper to see if she's right.

clap along
from 3 years

Clapping games help to develop a sense of rhythm and can get children used to counting to a beat.

- Sit opposite your child and get used to clapping in time with each other.
- Clap to the count of ten, saying a number out loud each time you clap.
- Clap out the syllables of your child's name. Repeat this several times, saying the name at different speeds.
- Finally, clap out some simple phrases, such as 'teddy has a woolly jumper', and count how many syllables there are in each one.

noisy animals!
from 4 years

This noisy animal game shows your child how to clap in simple rhythms.

- Show your child how to clap three times, pause, clap another three times, pause and so on.
- Now make animal noises in groups of three, for example, 'woof, woof, woof', and ask your child to clap in time.
- Now make animal noises in groups of four and ask him to clap along.
- Swap roles so that your child makes the animal sounds.

musical chit-chat

from 3 years

Having a musical 'conversation' encourages your child to listen very carefully to the number of beats you are playing.

- Find two toy drums – one for you and one for your child. Alternatively, improvise with upturned saucepans.
- Bang one beat on your drum. Ask your child to reply with one beat.
- Beat two times on your drum and ask your child to reply once again.
- Gradually increase the number of beats you want him to copy. Let him play some for you to copy too.
- If your child finds this hard, count the beats out loud as you play them.

RESEARCH SAYS

❛ **Music and rhythm are naturally comforting to children. Moving in time to music is an important form of non-verbal expression. It helps young children to express feelings that they don't yet have the language skills to vocalize.** ❜

Index